True Shoals Ghost Stories
Stories
Vol. 3

DEBRA GLASS

To Patricia Happy Hunting!

DEDICATION

To my readers who inspire me and so generously share their stories, to fellow history lovers, and to those who are thrilled by things that go bump in the night, this book is for you.

CONTENTS

ACKNOWLEDGMENTS

This book would not have been possible without the help of Bonnie Bak, Ed Balch, Amy Batton, Bobby Bugg, Sandra Calvert Terry, Mary Carton, Jason Cothrum, Bell Ezekiel, Micky Ezekiel, Lee Freeman, Jennifer George, IrixGuy, David Havens, Pat Bevis Kelly, Bonnie Carr Kerr, Heath Mathews, Gary Moody, John McWilliams, Jackie Quillen, Naima Simone, Keith Sims, and Brooke Sizemore.

Cover art by Tricia "Pickyme" Schmitt

Back cover author photo by Mary Carton

AUNT JENNY

Rich with mineral deposits, and situated in the foothills of the Appalachian Mountains, Winston County, Alabama has boasted a long and tumultuous history. A great portion of the 614 square mile county is home to one of four Alabama National Forests, the William B. Bankhead National Forest, named after US Representative William Brockman Bankhead from Lamar County Alabama, and father of noted actress, Tallulah Bankhead.

Winston County was originally established as Hancock County on February 12, 1850, and named for the famous signer of the Declaration of Independence, Massachusetts governor, John Hancock. But in 1858, the county was renamed Winston County in honor of Alabama governor, John A. Winston.

Just prior to the onset of the Civil War, when the states began seceding from the Union, Winston County elected a young, staunch Unionist schoolteacher named Christopher Sheats to represent the county at Alabama's secession convention. Once there, he rejected the secession ordinance, refusing to sign it. Sheats was expelled from the state legislature, and even imprisoned for treason.

This didn't dampen the spirits of Winston's *Tories*, those opposed to secession. They met at Looney's Tavern and passed three resolutions, lauding Sheats' determination, denying Alabama's right to secede, but stated that if Alabama had the right to leave the Union, then Winston County had the right to secede from the state.

To this day, some still refer to the county as the Republic of Winston, or the Free State of Winston.

Winston's secession from Alabama and the Confederacy was so well-known, it was mentioned in Harper Lee's *To Kill a Mockingbird.*

Because the rugged landscape is replete with steep hills and deep ravines, the terrain was ill-suited for cotton farming. Very few slave owners inhabited Winston County. Instead, the backbone of Winston's economy was made up of small-time, hard-scrabble farmers who struggled to cultivate the rough land.

When Winston County seceded from the Confederacy, its citizens hoped to remain neutral in the conflict between the North and South, however, the area became a hotbed of violence that lasted well after the war was over.

Confederate supporters sought to suppress the Unionist sympathizers in the area, and writs of arrest were issued throughout the county to those who were disloyal to the Southern Cause.

Those old enough to fight were conscripted by the Confederate government, but many fled, and still others helped Unionists escape to the safety of Federal lines to avoid being forced to fight for the South.

With many farms left unprotected, bands of Confederate foragers road roughshod through the hills and canyons, taking whatever they pleased, including food and livestock. These raiders often tortured and hanged Union sympathizers.

Sometime in late 1863 or early 1864, the Confederate Home Guard received word that a boot and saddle maker by the name of Willis Brooks Sr. was aiding Winston County Unionists.

A band of eight Confederates rode out to the tavern Brooks operated on Byler Road. There, they tortured and hanged Brooks, and when his eleven year-old son tried to intervene, one of the Confederates shot him dead.

It is said that Brooks' wife, a beautiful, blue-eyed, half Cherokee woman, Louisa Elisabeth Jane Bates—or Jenny, as she was known—gathered her young children and newborn baby around the two corpses and together, they bathed their hands in the blood of Willis Sr. and Willis Jr.

Jenny swore to avenge their deaths, and bade her sons to do the same. She pledged not to rest until all eight of the men responsible for her husband and son's deaths were killed.

Jenny taught her sons to shoot, and bragged in her later years that she'd "wasted many a keg of powder teaching my boys to shoot."

Louise Elizabeth Jane Bates

Of the eight Confederate raiders present that day, seven would pay with their lives, over the course of a thirty year feud, for their part in the murder of Willis Brooks and his son.

Legend attributes two of the men's deaths to Jenny herself. And when she killed their leader, she cut off his head, boiled it, and saved his skull to use as a soap dish.

Jenny, who became known as Aunt Jenny in the community where she lived, was said to have carried a hickory cane in which she cut a notch for each of the men her sons killed.

All of Jenny's ten sons were killed in their relentless quest for vengeance, and Jenny boasted that she was proud that all of her boys "died like men, with their boots on."

Aunt Jenny outlived every one of her sons. Family members claim that, on her deathbed, her pastor asked if there was anything he could do for her. She declared that she'd like to wash her hands. She was given a pan of water and the soap dish she'd made in 1864. She washed her hands one last time in the skull of the man she'd killed. When she dried her hands, she closed her eyes, and Aunt Jenny died on March 29, 1924, at the age of ninety-eight.

Aunt Jenny

But it seems Jenny's spirit is not at rest.

Those who visit the Bankhead National Forest and park near the old Brooks homestead tell tales of a ghostly woman, pounding on their windows with a cane, ordering them to get off her property, and threatening to kill them if they refuse. Before the hapless visitors can respond, the woman vanishes into thin air.

Others have witnessed a green light floating near the old home site and in the cemetery. Those brave enough to walk around the area have sensed an unearthly presence. Some have heard the footsteps of an unseen entity, crunching in the leaves.

Some visitors to the Brooks family cemetery leave coins at Aunt Jenny's grave because it was believed she was a witch, and that leaving the coins would bring them good luck. Jenny was referred to as a crone in her lifetime, and she would "lay hands" on the sick, as well as prepare herbal medicines which she dispensed to friends and relatives.

Coins left on Aunt Jenny's grave

Ghost hunters have recorded voices in the vicinity and have witnessed apparitions disappearing into the forest.

Sadly, vandals burned the house that was on the site and also ravaged the cemetery where Jenny is buried, stealing her headstone on several occasions.

If, by chance, you visit Bankhead National Forest, and come across the Brooks' home site and cemetery, pay your respects and maybe leave a few coins for Aunt Jenny. But know that you might encounter a restless spirit or two.

Perhaps Aunt Jenny's ghost is still in search of that one Confederate Home Guard rider who got away.

BOBBY

Postal employee, Bobby Bugg, flipped on the light switch in the basement of the Florence Post Office. An avid local history buff, he enjoyed coming to work early to pore through archival documents relating to the nearly century old building.

After all, legends abounded that the Florence Post Office actually belonged to the city of Florence, South Carolina, and that the plans for the post office Florence, Alabama received were ironically switched in the mail and the materials and blueprint for South Carolina's post office were sent to Alabama.

Though this tale has entertained the citizens of Florence for nearly a hundred years, there are no facts to support it.

In the early 1900s, Florence residents recognized the need for a Federal courthouse so they would not be forced to travel to either Huntsville or Birmingham for Federal court proceedings.

The site of the Florence Synodical Female College was chosen as the location for the new Federal building. The school was founded in 1855, by the Presbyterian Synod of Nashville, and its curriculum was designed to educate young women on their future roles as wives and hostesses.

The Florence Post Office in the early twentieth century

Florence Synodical Female College

A dormitory and academic building built by Zebulon Pike Morrison, who also built Wesleyan Hall, made up the campus which took up the entire city block between Seminary Street and Wood Avenue in Florence, as well as across Mobile Street from the First Presbyterian Church of Florence.

Dr. William Henry Mitchell served as president of the college until his death in 1872, and his tenure there was not without excitement.

On Sunday, July 27, 1862, Sallie Independence Foster, who was a thirteen year-old student at the Florence Synodical Female College, wrote the first entry in her journal: "It has been a really distressing day. The Yanks went into the Presbyterian Church and took Dr. Mitchell prisoner while he was praying and took him over the river, sent word to his wife that she must come to see him or she would not see him again."

Miss Foster was referring to the arrest of Dr. W. H. Mitchell, who pastored the First Presbyterian Church from 1851, to 1871.

Dr. W.H. Mitchell

Federal commanders routinely punished congregations if their clergy members preached against the Union Army, Federal government, or rallied church members in support of the Confederacy.

It was while such a mandate had been issued that Reverend Mitchell was arrested and imprisoned in Alton Penitentiary in Illinois for praying for Jefferson Davis and the success of the Confederate Army.

First Presbyterian Church 1930s

Mitchell was born in County Monaghan, Ireland in 1812. He was educated in Belfast and practiced law before immigrating to America in the 1840s. He attended Princeton University where he earned a doctorate in divinity. In 1843, he entered the ministry and pastored churches in Prattville, Wetumpka, and Montgomery, before coming to Florence in 1847, to serve as minister of the First Presbyterian Church.

R. T. Simpson, in his writings, recounted Dr. Mitchell's appearance, stating that he was "most impressed by his large blue eyes, his splendidly shaped head, and his earnest face."

First Presbyterian, the church Mitchell pastored at the time of his arrest, is, perhaps, the second oldest church in the state of Alabama, being built in 1818. The Presbyterians were the first church group to organize in the town of Florence and were also the first to build a place of worship. The church is located on its original site.

Although the church has undergone renovation, changing its looks, the outer walls of the 1824, building are the same ones which comprise the present-day sanctuary.

The first meeting house was a plain brick building with a white steeple, topped with a dome and a weather vane. The north face of the church was graced with a stained glass Palladian window. The interior had three rows of high pews with doors on each side. A special section was reserved for the slaves. The choir loft was in the rear, upper part of the sanctuary.

The church, as it appears today, is very similar to the original structure, although annexes have been added. Also, where the former front doors were, there are now two stained-glass transom windows. The old white steeple was destroyed and now there are two towers framing the façade.

W. H. Mitchell must have been proud of the Presbyterian meeting house and its congregation, which included General John Coffee, Governor Robert Miller Patton, the Honorable John McKinley, and their families.

Justice John B. McKinley for whom the Post Office was named

W. H. Mitchell became something of a local folk hero during the Civil War. On Sunday morning, July 27, 1862, he stepped into the pulpit and looked out across his congregation, which was interspersed with some of the occupying Union soldiers and, despite an mandate passed by the Federals against praying for the

Confederacy, said a prayer for President Jefferson Davis and for the success of the Confederate Armies.

After the "Amen" was sounded, Colonel John Marshall Harlan, Provost Marshal of the 10th Kentucky Regiment and future Associate Justice of the US Supreme Court, got up from his pew, strode up to the pulpit and told Dr. Mitchell that the service should cease at once, and that he should consider himself a prisoner of the United States Army.

Then, to the horror of Mitchell's congregation, he was placed under guard, marched across the Tennessee River to Tuscumbia, and put on a train to Alton, Illinois where he spent four months in Federal prison.

It is believed that some members of the church followed Mitchell to the railroad station in Tuscumbia. Sallie Foster wrote in her journal, "They would not let him joist his umbrella. They said he could stand the sun as well as they could."

Relatives and friends intervened on Mitchell's behalf and secured his release. Sallie's journal entry on Sunday morning, October 12, 1862, stated that Dr. Mitchell had returned home and had resumed his position as pastor of First Presbyterian and as president of the Synodical College. His congregation dubbed him the "prison pastor."

He resigned his pastorate in 1871, and died on October 2, 1872. He was buried in the cemetery at the Forks of Cypress. A memorial window graces the sanctuary of the First Presbyterian Church in Mitchell's honor.

Alabama Governor, Robert M. Patton, served as president of the Synodical College from 1872 until 1873.

The college closed its doors in 1893, but the building was leased to the Reverend A. H. Todd, who ran a private institution on the campus until 1897.

In November 1911, the school was torn down and the Barnes Brothers of Logansport, Indiana began excavation to ready the site for the post office. Plans were drawn up by architect, James K. Taylor, a cousin of Hiram Kennedy-Douglass, whose ancestors were among the founding fathers of Florence.

Florence citizens were excited as the grand structure took shape. The stairways were honed from Alabama marble, and tiles were custom-made from Georgia marble for the floors. Doors and openings were trimmed in oak. And when the Neo-Classical building was completed, Post-master C. W. Moore hosted an open house October 17, 1913.

In 1999, and through the tireless work of William Smith, the post office was renamed for Justice John McKinley, a founding father of Florence, who served as a senator and representative from Alabama. President Martin Van Buren appointed him Associate Justice of the United States Supreme Court in April 1837, a post he held until his death in 1852.

It was this sort of history that fascinated Bobby Bugg, and while he sat in the basement of the post office one morning, around 3 a.m., he heard a woman's voice.

"Bobby!" the voice called.

He peered into the dark hallway. "I'm in the basement!" He waited for a response, but got none and went back to his research.

Moments later, he heard the voice again. "Bobby!"

This time, he stood and went to the door. "I'm in the basement," he called back, and listened.

One more time, the woman's voice cried his name. Thinking perhaps one of the other employees hadn't heard him, he climbed the stairs. Darkness shadowed the marble-tiled entry way. Seeing no one, Bobby ventured to the mail sorting room where two other postal employees were working.

"What'd you need?" he asked.

The workers seemed confused. "What do you mean?" one asked.

"Didn't you call me?" Bobby asked the female employee.

"No."

"I could have sworn I heard someone calling my name," Bobby explained.

"No one called you. We've been in here since we clocked in," the male told him.

Suddenly, the female's face paled. Her eyes widened. "I know who was calling you," she said, "It was Bobby Isley's mother, looking for son."

A chill crawled up Bobby Bugg's spine. He knew the story of Bobby Isley very well.

On February 11, 1960, eleven year old Bobby Wayne Isley and two friends visited the Navy Recruiting office on the second floor of the post office, looking for book marks and other souvenirs. On their way back down the stairs, Bobby leaned over the railing and fell to his death on the marble floor below.

His mother, Velma Isley, was said to have never recovered from the loss of her beloved son. She followed him in death, passing away from a broken heart, a mere two years after the accident that claimed Bobby's life. Mother and son are buried in adjoining plots in Tri-Cities Memorial Gardens.

Longtime USPS employee, Jackie Quillen, refuses to go to the basement alone.

Other employees have heard a woman's voice around the same time in the post office, and have also experienced hearing equipment being moved in the building when no one else is present. Doors open and close of their own accord, and the water in the ladies' room often turns on by itself.

And one time, several employees witnessed one of the heavy mail bins rolling across the floor.

Though no apparitions have ever been seen in the historic building, the inexplicable events experienced by those who work there in the wee hours of the morning leave them with the feeling they're not alone.

Could the spirit of Velma Isley still wander the marble-tiled floors where her son's life came to a horrible and untimely end? Or could the presence stem from the turbulent Civil War era, when a vibrant college occupied the site where the Florence's post office now stands?

SMITHSONIA MANSION

While most citizens of North Alabama struggled during the bitter years of the Reconstruction Era, there was one entrepreneur who turned a fledgling ferry operation, in a small community known then as Cave Spring, into a thriving agricultural center that would be renamed in his honor.

His name was Columbus Smith. But those who knew him well, referred to him as Pad Smith.

Cave Spring was established roughly thirteen miles west of Florence, on the banks of the Tennessee River, in the early nineteenth century, when Christopher Cheatham launched a ferry service.

Cheatham's ferry was a few miles upriver from the ferry operated by Chickasaw Chief George Colbert where the Natchez Trace crossed the Tennessee River. After Cheatham passed away, the property and ferry passed down to his daughter, Martha Ann Rowell, who sold the ferry operation and land to a Franklin County man named D. C. Oats. In July 1863, the seventy acres of land and ferry rights were purchased by Columbus Smith and his step-father John Richards.

Smith became sole owner of the acreage and ferry in August 1867, for a total price of $3,500.00. He paid far more for the ferry rights than the land.

Columbus Smith (center) with family

As most Southerners grappled with economic insecurity, Columbus Smith thrived. He opened a country store near his ferry which proved to be an advantage for him as he had built-in customers. Smith also rented out portions of his land to sharecroppers, both black and white. Most of the time, little to no cash changed hands. Instead the sharecroppers traded their corn and cotton for supplies from Smith's store.

By 1886, the town of Smithsonia had expanded to such a size that the community required its own post office. Columbus Smith was appointed the first postmaster on May 5, 1886, when he was fifty-three-years old.

At its height, Smith's empire consisted of the ferry, the store, a grist mill, cotton gin, and several other small businesses required of a small community. By 1900, Smith owned nearly 10,000 acres of land, and was one of the largest principal land owners in Lauderdale County, and the county's greatest taxpayer.

Smith married Permelia Carroll in May 1867. She passed away in 1874, at only twenty-five. Two years later, Smith remarried a woman named Martha Young. The couple had four sons and three daughters. One named Annie passed away as a child.

Smith built a small two-room house near the ferry where he lived until 1876, when he built a six-room frame house. However, as his wealth increased, so did his standard of living.

Martha Ann Young Smith

In the 1880s, he built a grand, eleven-room, three-story mansion on the banks overlooking the Tennessee River. The house was constructed of cut stone, fitted with all the modern conveniences of the time, and decorated with furniture purchased abroad. A massive bell graced the cupola atop the structure.

His daughter, Bessie Smith Reeder, recalled the move to the new house in a March 31, 1963, *Florence Times* article. "It was on January 1, 1885. I was five years old. The nurse drove the buggy and my baby brother sat between the two of us."

Family stories and legends still abound of a giant cave that stretched from the Tennessee River, beneath the house, where the Smiths and their friends held great parties on a spacious, flat ledge close to the mouth of the cave. Several of the cave's chambers were named for those various features. The entrance was said to have been around forty feet in width, and a Waterloo teacher named John Lincoln Hall Sr., explored the cave, estimating that he and his companions traveled several miles into the cavern, describing it as an underground river.

Smithsonia Mansion 1960

Some of the legends associated with the cave stem from the time of Hernando DeSoto's conquest of Alabama. In 1971, near the Natchez Trace Bridge in Colbert County, two men discovered a brick-sized gold ingot. A farmer tending a field just south of Smithsonia found a gold bar that had either Indian or Spanish markings.

Behind the house, in the fertile farming area known as the Bend of the River, stretched acre upon acre of cotton fields, and below the house, Smith's steamboats lined the riverbank.

After Smith's death on July 9, 1900, he was buried in the antebellum cemetery at Canaan Methodist Church.

Some of the property passed down to his daughter, Bessie Smith Reeder and her husband, John Thomas Reeder, who managed the estate for many years.

Smithsonia Mansion early twentieth century

Reeder, as it happened, was married to two of the Smith sisters, the first being Lizzie Smith, whom he married in 1888, and who died in 1897, and then Bessie Smith.

Reeder, who followed in his father-in-law's footsteps as postmaster of Smithsonia, was a Notary Public, a Master Mason, a Knight of Pythias, a member of B.P.O.E., and was a trustee of the Lauderdale County school system. Reeder owned the Tennessee River Packet Company, and operated several small steamboats that transported goods and passengers back and forth to Florence.

Bessie Smith Reeder was interviewed by Lorene Frederick in the *Florence Times*, March 31, 1963. "Oh, it would just thrill me to hear a steamboat whistle again," she told Ms. Frederick. After all, Bessie Reeder had grown up thinking the Tennessee was "daddy's river."

The stone mansion ended up in the hands of Columbus Smith's son, Jefferson Smith, who was said to have owned the first automobile in the area. According to an article by Tom Johnson for the *Montgomery Independent*, entitled *With a Sigh, Not a Whimper*, Jeff Smith "could be seen coming by his plumes of dust—alarming old ladies, agitating the livestock, and scaring the hell out of chickens."

Johnson went on to indicate that Jeff Smith lived alone, inhabiting only two rooms of the stone mansion, in the 1930s. By this time, Pickwick Lake had been flooded, and the once verdant valley below the house now served as the bed of the Tennessee River. Jeff Smith utilized the first floor of the house as his living quarters. The second had been a ballroom, and the third was described by Tom Johnson as an orchestra pit.

Tales flourished that Columbus Smith had installed a grand piano on the third floor.

In the early twentieth century, as transportation became more affordable, Smithsonia's river empire began to decline, and when TVA acquired the shoreline and began clearing the land in order to build dams, the remainder of Smith's operations were torn down to make way for the expanded lake.

As Jeff Smith's inheritance dwindled, he moved inland to a smaller house, leaving Columbus Smith's grand stone mansion to local tenant farmers.

It was during this time that Bell Woods married Fred Ezekiel, and moved into the mansion along with her family. Bell and her husband occupied the second story rooms, while her parents and sister lived in the first floor rooms.

Often, when Bell was alone in the cavernous house, she would hear the front door open and close, but upon investigation, would find no one there. Inexplicable cold spots sent shivers up her spine, even during the sultry Alabama summers when there was otherwise no respite from the oppressive heat.

The sound of mysterious footsteps traversing the wood floors was prevalent.

Sometimes, the faint strains of piano music could be heard wafting from the cupola, where Bell and her family never dared to go.

One night, when everyone was asleep in the house, Bell was awakened by a blood-curdling scream. She bolted upright in the bed, listening in the darkness, her heart hammering as footsteps raced up the stairs.

Her nightgown clad sister appeared in the doorway, illuminated only by the moonlight streaming through the window. "There was a man," she rasped breathlessly, glancing with trepidation back toward the stairs.

"What man?" Bell asked, alarmed.

Trembling uncontrollably, the sister continued. "I woke up and saw a man bending over me as if he were going to pick me up."

"You were dreaming. Go back to bed," Bell told her.

The sister shook her head. "No. He woke me up, and when he reached for me, I screamed. And then...he...he vanished."

Neither of them ever saw the man again, but Bell believed her sister, because she, herself, had always felt the presence of the stone mansion's former inhabitants, as if they remained, unseen, the ghostly lords and ladies of a bygone feudal kingdom.

Those brave enough to walk the riverbank at night, have claimed to hear the eerie blare of a steamboat whistle drifting across the dark waters.

One tenant farmer who lived in the house told a tale that he was on his way home from town in his horse-drawn buggy one night in the vicinity of the Smith Mansion, and a ghost appeared on the seat next to him, rode awhile and then vanished. He and his family also heard footsteps coming from the upstairs, but could find no explanation.

The cave, and most of Columbus Smith's enterprise is now underwater, and has been since the flooding of Pickwick Lake in the late 1930s.

A special edition of the *Florence Times* in 1900, summed up Columbus Smith's life and legacy best. "His qualifications were not those of heraldic blazonry, nor of genealogy, nor of medieval ancestry, but of common everyday pluck and push joined to an indomitable spirit that laughed at momentary clouds of disaster and that scored the senility of the past and gone."

Smith's stone mansion was completely abandoned sometime during the late 1960s.

One frequent visitor to Smithsonia Mansion, Bonnie Carr Kerr, described the forsaken manor. Two brick out-buildings served as the kitchen and pantry. Some of the walls in the mansion had already collapsed, but when she first explored the house, the floorboards were still intact on the first and second floors. Large plaster rosettes graced the ceilings where grand light fixtures had once hung. The walnut window frames had been removed and installed in a new house being built. The stairwell stretched up from the foyer, however the treads and risers had been removed by vandals. The closets had been wallpapered with old newspapers, and even as the stone façade crumbled, the beautiful tiled mantles remained, a testament to a time when the house represented Southern perseverance and charm—a time long before its deserted and moldering rooms were claimed by the ghosts.

Recent photo of Smithsonia Mansion ruins courtesy of Bonnie Carr Kerr

HENRY'S HILL

Just past Rock Springs Church, where County Road 448 makes a sharp curve and turns into County Road 25, there's a stretch of pavement that looks like any other hill on any other country lane. Chicken houses dot the undulating landscape. Cows graze in fenced-in pastures. Trees and bushes line the road.

Henry's Hill near Mt. Hope, Alabama

In fact, there doesn't appear to be anything remarkable about the place.

Except that the road is said to be haunted by the Good Samaritan ghost of a man known only as Henry.

According to popular legend, Henry and his family were traveling along County Road 25, and just after he made the sharp turn, his car broke down. Fearing a speeding driver would come around the curve and hit the car, he and his eldest son got out to push their vehicle out of the road.

Henry had forgotten to disengage the parking brake, and just as he stepped around the car, another vehicle rounded the corner and struck Henry, killing him instantly.

Ever since that fateful day, those who stall at the base of the hill, have witnessed an unseen force, pushing their car up the rise to safety.

Many skeptics have visited the hill, stopped at the dip where local lore states Henry was killed, have turned off their engines, put their cars in neutral, and have sat in awe as their vehicles began to roll uphill.

While some attribute the mysterious ascending movement of their cars to a helpful spirit, others claim the phenomenon is merely an optical illusion.

A few visitors to the hill, however, left convinced they perceived more than a trick of the eye.

One group of travelers along the road decided to test the theory late one evening, and even dusted their trunk with baby powder. They all claim to have seen a black figure with bony fingers and red eyes approach their car before they began the ascent up the hill. And when they got up the nerve to check the powder-coated trunk, they were shocked to discover handprints on the back of their car.

A young man named Justin and his father stopped at the top of the hill, and when they stepped out of their car, they heard what sounded like a young girl screaming. They left, but returned later, and heard the same shriek again. Attempts to record the sound proved unsuccessful.

A Shoals native who chronicles his adventures as IrixGuy, recounted his 1999 experience with the ghost of Henry in his YouTube video entitled *Henry's Hill (haunted hill) in Mt Hope, Alabama – EVP, Orb & Apparition Captured.*

According to IrixGuy, some friends suggested they ride out to Henry's Hill one night to see if the tales they'd heard were true. IrixGuy, who was a skeptic, went along.

The driver stopped in the ruts in the road, at the bottom of the hill, switched off the ignition, and shifted into neutral. What IrixGuy beheld next changed his mind about the spirit world.

He said they felt a definite push coming from the rear of the car, and then the vehicle began to slowly travel up the hill.

He recounted the story to his parents the next day, and together they visited Henry's Hill. With IrixGuy in the driver's seat, they tested the phenomenon. Sure enough, the car was pushed and moved of its own accord uphill about fifty feet.

Wanting to experience it for himself, IrixGuy's father switched places and climbed into the driver's seat. IrixGuy stood outside the car to watch.

But as long as he watched, nothing happened. "If this was gravity, it should work regardless of whether or not someone is staring at the rear of the vehicle," he stated in his video.

He returned to the car, and once he was inside, the car began to move up the hill again, but stopped short of how far it had traveled before. Then, coming from the back of the car, IrixGuy's mother heard a distinct gasping sound as if someone were trying to catch their breath.

IrixGuy heard heavy boot steps on the pavement, moving from the rear of the car to the passenger side door. Moments later, the vehicle began to move uphill again. He described feeling the fine hairs on the back of his neck standing on end. And then, without warning, an otherworldly scream rent the air that seemed as if it were coming from inside the vehicle.

Though IrixGuy vowed never to return to Henry's Hill, he's since made several trips to the location, and has observed temperature fluctuations, noticed that the cows in the pasture seem to grow restless whenever a car stops on the road, and describes the site as being unusually windy, even during calm weather.

He has sprinkled his trunk with baby powder to see if handprints will appear, but without success.

However, he has gotten spikes on his EMF meter, which ghost hunters use to record changes in electromagnetic frequencies, and has photographed orbs, and even an apparition who appears to be wearing a hat and long-sleeved shirt.

His evidence can be seen on his YouTube channel, IrixGuy's Adventure Channel. www.YouTube.com/IrixGuy

Though there is no concrete proof a man named Henry was ever killed at the location, road crews have been unable to keep the ruts in the road filled at the bottom of Henry's Hill. Efforts to level the spot are futile because the depression will appear mere days after workers attempt to smooth out the road.

If it is true that Henry died on County Road 25, he might not be the only spirit haunting the country lane.

Mount Hope, Alabama was the backdrop for Streight's Raid, a Civil War campaign executed by Union Colonel Abel D. Streight to forage and destroy portions of the railroad.

In March 1863, Streight set out on a mounted cavalry raid across North Alabama and into Georgia, in hopes of cutting off supply lines to the Confederate Army of Tennessee.

Federal Colonel Abel D. Streight

Lacking horses, many of Streight's men were forced to ride mules commandeered from Tennessee farms. Wherever they rode, amused Southerners were quick to hurl insults at the slow-moving brigade, dubbing them the "Jackass Cavalry."

By April, Streight and his men rode into Tuscumbia, Alabama, but were engaged in a series of hot skirmishes commanded by

Confederate General Nathan Bedford Forrest and Colonel Phillip Roddey.

Heavy rains halted the Jackass Brigade in Mount Hope where they remained to scour the country for horses and mules. About three miles west of the town, Streight's men stopped at Dr. L. N. Templeton's plantation where they dragged his family's piano to the barn, gutted it, and used the hull as a feed trough for their mules.

The Cunningham family suffered a similar fate at the hands of the Federals. In Nancy Cunningham's 1905 account of the incident, she wrote, "We moved into a couple of old houses that stood down in the field. They were very sorry and shabby looking cabins, but they were a shelter, and I felt that their ordinary appearance would make the Yankees think we were so poverty stricken they would feel sorry for us and not molest us."

The Cunninghams hid their valuables in a hollow log, and their horses in the hills, but the Federals discovered them and took everything they could carry.

General Nathan Bedford Forrest, CSA

While in Mount Hope, Streight's men were involved in several bloody skirmishes with squads of Confederate cavalrymen.

Confederate Lt. Colonel John W. Estes wrote of the devastation Mount Hope suffered during Streight's Raid. "In a word, this district is almost destitute of subsistence for man or beast. There is not corn enough in this valley to support the citizens if there were no troops here."

Estes added, "Many families are compelled to suffer or leave here if some means of transporting subsistence is not provided."

Other eye witnesses to the Federal occupation also left accounts. After the war, Hodge L. Stephenson wrote that Federal troops stole money from the estate of James Wallace, who died in 1858. Wallace, who had no children, had left part of his estate for a schoolhouse in Mount Hope. "During the late disastrous Civil War, he was robbed by the Federal soldiers under Col. Streight," Stephenson recounted, and went on to report that the "enemy" stole at least $2,500.00, if not a larger sum from Wallace's estate.

Forrest deviled Streight across the state, and on May 2, 1863, Streight crossed Black Creek about three miles from Gadsden. He burned the bridge behind him, hoping to put some distance between his brigade and Forrest's seasoned horsemen.

Forrest was met by a young sixteen-year-old girl named Emma Sansom, who guided him to a ford where his men could safely cross the swollen creek.

Emma Sansom

Forrest's cavalry surrounded Streight at Cedar Bluff where the Federal brigade was forced to surrender. Streight's attempts to disrupt Confederate supply lines failed.

Perhaps Henry's Hill was the site of a skirmish during those turbulent Civil War years. Or maybe the legends told about a man who died, trying to push his family to safety are true.

Perhaps the skeptics are right about the hill being an optical illusion which would account for how vehicles move uphill, seemingly unaided.

But those who've explored the location all have their own theories.

If you'd like to find out for yourself, drive to the sharp curve where County Road 448 turns into County Road 25, park in the dip in the pavement, shift into neutral, and see what happens.

THE JAZZ MAN

Just east of Elgin, Alabama, Highway 72 crosses Second Creek, a tributary of Wheeler Lake. This bridge is like many others in the Tennessee Valley, a scenic crossing where travelers might view boats, cranes, and even tortoises sunning on the banks.

A favorite spot for local fishermen, this area offers the greatest population of smallmouth bass on the Tennessee River. Bluffs, river ledges, submerged stumps, gravel bars, milfoil grass, and numerous creeks create plentiful hiding spots the prized fish. Even long-forgotten road beds lie beneath the murky waters.

In 2002, Jimmy Mason won the American Bass Association National Championship in the area.

The stretch between Elgin and Rogersville, Alabama is rich with history. This area was once claimed by two Native American tribes prevalent in North Alabama: the Cherokees and the Chickasaws. The remains of a Native American village could once be seen just southwest of Center Star, about five miles west of Elgin. Just one mile east, near the Second Creek Bridge, there is an area known as the "Indian Mound."

The Elgin community was settled by early pioneers around 1833, and has been called various names: Middleton and Elgin, and Ingram's Elgin Crossroads. A town called Covington was established on the northern bank of Second Creek.

Second Creek got its name as early as 1817. It flows into Lauderdale County from Lawrence County, Tennessee, and meanders through farmland southward where it converges with the Tennessee River.

On the east side of the creek, Felix Johnson, a citizen of Covington, organized the Goodsprings Cumberland Presbyterian Church on a tree-covered knoll. A spot next to the church was designated for the cemetery.

The Covington community thrived until 1936, when construction on Wheeler Dam was completed and the citizens were ordered to evacuate the area. By 1937, water covered most of Covington's farms and thoroughfares. The one lane steel bridge that had crossed Second Creek was moved upstream to another location, and a new highway was built with a causeway connecting the site of the old bridge, thereby providing a two-lane highway across the creek.

While the church became Goodsprings Baptist, and moved to the Thornton community, the original cemetery remains at the old location on Second Creek.

In the 1970s, Highway 72 was widened into four lanes, and each day, thousands of cars traverse the bridge, most without incident.

However, there are some who've driven across the bridge on foggy nights only to see a man, wearing a white suit and hat, standing in the middle of the westbound lane.

Those who've stopped to help or offer him a ride, claim he approaches the car and asks the passengers if they've seen his trumpet. Before they can respond, he vanishes.

The mysterious musician is known only as the Jazz Man, and legend holds that he was struck by a car and killed one foggy night in the 1940s, as he was walking home from a gig.

Witnesses to the apparition assert that he wears a white Zoot Suit, a man's suit with high-waisted, wide-legged, tight-cuffed trousers and a long coat with overly large lapels and wide padded shoulders.

One person maintained that he and a passenger were driving onto the bridge when they both noticed an odd fog, and then a man standing in the right hand lane appeared as if he materialized out of the mist itself.

As they slowed down, they could see his hat, face, and the Zoot Suit, but as they neared, he evaporated into the fog.

It's safe to surmise the Jazz Man probably lived during the early 1940s, since he is always seen in the style so iconic to the music scene of that era.

Zoot Suits attained popularity among musicians during the big band era, and the name *Zoot Suit* has been attributed to Harold C. Fox, a Chicago clothier and trumpet player in a big band.

Sparking riots across the country, the Zoot Suit was banned during WWII due to the enormous amount of fabric used in the suit's construction. Wearers believed the suits themselves were a declaration of freedom and rebelliousness.

One trademark of the suit was the fedora or pork pie hat which was color-coordinated to the suit and often adorned with a feather.

Another was the long watch chain which dangled from the belt to the knee or below, then stretched back upward to the side pocket.

A young Malcolm X described the trend as "a killer-diller coat with a drape shape, reet pleats, and shoulders padded like a lunatic's cell."

Cab Calloway sported a Zoot Suit in the 1943 film, *Stormy Weather*.

We might not ever know the true identity of the Jazz Man who haunts Second Creek Bridge, but if you happen to drive along that isolated stretch of road on a foggy night, you might see the wandering, Zoot Suit-clad spirit, in search of his long lost trumpet.

ALBA WOOD PLANTATION

The fertile farm land, about eleven miles west of Florence, known as the Bend of the River, was the location of several antebellum plantations. And while some of those are still in existence, many have been lost to history.

Archeological research indicates that an earlier structure once stood on the site Pope's Tavern Museum now occupies. It is believed this building was constructed by one of North Alabama's pioneer settlers, Christopher Cheatham, in the early 1810s, and that it served as the first inn and stagecoach stop in Florence, Alabama. At that time, the region was still inhabited by the Native American Cherokee and Chickasaw tribes.

Cheatham had operated the Twickenham Hotel in Huntsville, Alabama, and was partial owner of Huntsville's historic Bell Tavern, where such notables as Andrew Jackson and Davy Crockett stayed in 1813. The bell which prompted the name Bell Tavern is now preserved in the Alabama Department of Archives and History, though the original structure burned in 1855.

After moving to Cave Spring, roughly thirteen miles west of Florence, Cheatham launched a ferry service on the banks of the

Tennessee River, in the area now known as Smithsonia.

He also owned several acres of land which he dubbed Alba Wood, pronounced *Al-luh-bah Wood*.

According to *Alba Wood's Rich History*, a November 30, 2000, article in the *Times Daily* newspaper, written by Florence City Historian, Bill McDonald, the name Alba Wood, was an ancient Celtic word that meant "wood of Scotland."

Cheatham's ferry was a few miles upriver from the ferry operated by Chickasaw Chief George Colbert where the Natchez Trace crossed the Tennessee River.

Cheatham lived in a log house on his Alba Wood plantation, and died there, January 10, 1816. He is buried in the Rowell Cemetery on the former grounds of the plantation that fronts Gunwaleford Road.

After Cheatham passed away, the property and ferry passed down to his daughter, Martha Ann Rowell, who sold the ferry operation and land to a Franklin County man named D. C. Oats, who hailed from the Newport Plantation in Colbert County, Alabama, and was the first postmaster of Cherokee, Alabama.

Christopher Cheatham's grave, Rowell Cemetery

After inheriting Cheatham's plantation, Martha Ann and her husband, a physician named Neal Rowell, began construction on a mansion in the early 1840s.

Martha Ann Smith Rowell

Surrounded by vast tracts of cotton and corn fields, the new manor house stood atop a knoll. Constructed in the English Bond design, the house featured solid brick walls with a foundation of yellow poplar logs. Alba Wood's most striking feature was the crow-stepped gables with double chimneys on the side walls. Similar architectural features can be seen at Wakefield on North Court Street, and Hickory Place on North Pine Street, in Florence.

The Rowells were among the wealthiest landowners in Lauderdale County. An 1850 census indicated that Rowell owned seventy-two slaves, generated 180,000 pounds of cotton per year, and was worth roughly $101,000.00, approximately three million by today's standards.

By 1860, Rowell possessed ninety slaves.

Neal Rowell was born November 14, 1796, in Wood City, Virginia. He became a prominent physician after moving to Lauderdale County, and married Martha Ann Cheatham, who was fifteen years his junior, on December 6, 1832.

Neal Rowell

Rowell was known for his intellectual pursuits, and he had a large library at Alba Wood. One of his most prized possessions was a gun that had belonged to his father, Dr. Daniel Rowell, who had married Nancy Ann Neal, the daughter of Revolutionary War Captain James Neal.

Daniel Rowell had stashed the gun, emblazoned with the inscription "Liberty or Death," in a hollow log after being set upon by Native Americans. The gun was found some sixty-seven years later, the muzzle grown into the trunk of a dogwood tree. The barrel, trigger, guard, thimble, and brass cover bearing the words "Liberty of Death," were sent to Neal Rowell in 1859, around eight years after Daniel Rowell passed away at Alba Wood at the age of 93.

For all of the respect Dr. Neal Rowell garnered, he was not without legal troubles. On October 1, 1845, he was indicted, in Lauderdale County, for assault and battery. No other details of the case are known.

Neal Rowell passed away December 6, 1886, at ninety years old.

Neal Rowell's grave, Rowell Cemetery

On July 29, 1886, six months prior to Neal Rowell's death, *The Winston Herald* reported a murder at Alba Wood. "There was an atrocious murder in Colbert's Reserve on the plantation of Dr. Neal Rowell, last Saturday, about 11 o'clock. Two servants, Henry Brock, aged 20 years, and John Marks, aged 12, were plowing together in the field, no one else being present. Under these circumstances and surrounding, the murder was committed with no one but the principals to witness. After the deed was committed, Brock went to the house and informed Marks' family that Marks had been kicked by his mule and killed. The boy was found dead in the field and his face covered by his hat. Fortunately, for justice, Captain E. B. Thompson happened to be present when the murdered boy was brought in, and made an examination of the body so as to find the nature of his injuries and was horrified to find a small bullet hole in his left breast. Brock, upon being questioned strenuously denied any knowledge of how it was caused, but when carried to the spot where the murder had been committed, he showed where he had buried the pistol in the earth after committing the dastardly crime. In the preliminary trial, evidence was introduced, showing that he had stated several times previous to committing the crime his intention of murdering the boy. He was tried before Squire W. B. Bayless, brought to Florence, and placed in jail by Constable George Hale to await the action of the grand jury. It was a cowardly and contemptible crime, and his swift hanging will be only a just retribution meted out to him by the laws which he has outraged."

Martha Ann Cheatham Rowell died July 13, 1890. She outlived all but one of her children.

Alba Wood, which had been carved out of a wilderness once roamed by Native American and Spanish explorers, had witnessed occupation by both armies during the Civil War, and had survived the ravages of the Reconstruction Era, fell into the hands of descendants who eventually leased the manor house to tenant farmers during the early twentieth century.

Bell Woods Ezekiel recalls living in the house as a child, and maintains many inexplicable events occurred while she and her family resided there.

The house could be seen for a great distance down the

Gunwaleford Road, and Bell said that often, when the family had been to town, upon returning, light blazed from every window of the two story mansion. However, when they arrived at the house, they found it dark. Thinking someone had been there, they checked to see if the lightbulbs were hot, but found none even warm.

Martha Rowell's grave, Rowell Cemetery

Just before Bell was married, she, her mother, and baby sister sat in an upstairs room while Mrs. Woods sewed. A baby's cry echoed through the downstairs rooms of the house, but Bell found no reasonable explanation for the sound.

Doors often flew open as if pushed by unseen hands.

On more than one occasion, Bell heard the sound of horse hooves on the first story floorboards.

Her sister was terrified when she encountered a ghostly woman on the back porch, wearing a white antebellum style dress.

Other tenants professed to have discovered money buried under the kitchen floor. Tales were whispered that during the war years, three servants had been blindfolded and carted around the countryside, only to be brought back to the house where, still blindfolded, they were instructed to dig a hole where the family valuables were to be buried. When one of the servants peeked, he was killed.

Bell believed the tales because she said a dark stain, that could not be cleaned, marred the floorboards in the dining room.

Mr. Woods scoured the ground in the crawlspace beneath the house, but alas found no buried treasure, and yet Bell believes the ghosts at Alba Wood remained to guard riches yet to be unearthed.

Tragically, the once grand manor sank into a state of disrepair and was abandoned altogether. The ruins fell victim to a bulldozer, and cotton fields reclaimed the knoll where the house stood sentinel over Alba Wood.

Travelers along Gunwaleford Road still sometimes see mysterious lights and ghostly figures on the knoll, all that is left of where Alba Wood once stood.

THE SPIRIT OF MUSCLE SHOALS SOUND

Sweet Home Alabama by Lynyrd Skynyrd is indisputably the most popular Southern anthem of all time. But one line has been frequently misquoted since the song's release in June 1974. Many sing the lyrics, "Muscle Shoals has got the swamplands."

And even though the city in Northwest Alabama is situated on the banks of the Tennessee River, the lyrics are actually: "Now Muscle Shoals has got the Swampers. And they've been known to pick a song or two."

The Swampers was the nickname given to the Muscle Shoals Rhythm Section, by producer, Denny Cordell during a session for singer/songwriter, Leon Russell, due to the "swampy sound," a distinctive flavor that can only be described as a blend of gritty rhythm and blues and country soul prevalent in rock music throughout the 1960s and 1970s.

In the early 1960s, the Swampers—David Hood, Barry Beckett, Roger Hawkins, Jimmy Johnson, Clayton Ivey, Spooner Oldham, and others—worked as session musicians who backed music greats including Aretha Franklin, Wilson Pickett, Arthur Alexander, Otis Redding, Clarence Carter, Etta James, and Percy Sledge among others at Fame Recording Studio in Muscle Shoals, Alabama.

At a time when Alabama held the reputation as the most racially tense state in the country, the all-white Swampers and Fame founder and producer, Rick Hall, created an unmistakably black sound— music with deep spiritual roots that would soon blur the lines of race, and serve to bring together two cultures that had been segregated since American colonial times.

When Rick Hall opened the doors to Fame, the nearest music studios were in Memphis and Nashville, so Hall had his pick of local talent that music producer, Jerry Wexler, would later describe as "white boys who took a left turn at the blues."

At the time when Arthur Alexander recorded *You Better Move On* at Fame, the white studio musicians and black singers could not have sat down at the same table in a restaurant in Alabama. In the studio, however, color ceased to be an issue.

After a rift between Aretha Franklin's husband and manager, Ted White, and Rick Hall, following a recording session, four of the founding Swampers—bassist, David Hood, keyboardist, Barry Beckett, drummer, Roger Hawkins, and guitarist, Jimmy Johnson— decided to launch their own studio, Muscle Shoals Sound, in an unassuming brick building at 3614 Jackson Highway in Sheffield, Alabama. The building is rumored to have once been used to store headstones and grave slabs for the cemetery across the street, and legends have flourished that at one time, it was a business that sold or manufactured coffins.

"It was like being entombed," Swamper, Jimmy Johnson, described the virtually windowless building in *Deep Soul: How Muscle Shoals Became Music's Most Unlikely Hit Factory*, an article by Mick Brown for *The Telegraph*.

But artists clamored for the mythical Muscle Shoals sound, and traveled from all corners of the world to the sleepy little town on the banks of the Tennessee River. Among the first was a British band known as The Rolling Stones, who cut hits *Brown Sugar* and *Wild Horses*, for their *Sticky Fingers* album, on December 3-4, 1969, at the studio. In fact, it is said that Keith Richards wrote *Wild Horses* in the studio's cramped bathroom.

In a June 8, 2015 interview for *USA Today*, Richards remembers Muscle Shoals Sound. "A lot of good music was coming out of there. Every record, you'd say, 'Where was that recorded?' It would turn out to be Muscle Shoals. We took a little week off and said, 'We've got to try this room out.'"

An excerpt from *Rocks Off, 50 Tracks That Tell the Story of The Rolling Stones* by Bill Janovitz, states: "Keith and Mick stood at the same microphone at Muscle Shoals, lights dimmed, splitting a fifth of bourbon, and simultaneously sang the melodies and harmonies on the three songs they had recorded over three days: *Brown Sugar*, *You Got to Move*, and *Wild Horses*. That's your rock'n'roll fantasy right there, pal: A six-piece band working in a tiny converted coffin factory across from an Alabama graveyard, on an eight track recorder, with no computer editing or Autotune, recorded three songs representing 30 percent of one of the greatest rock'n'roll records of all time."

Muscle Shoals Sound Studio, Sheffield, Alabama

Muscle Shoals Sound Studio

Other artists who recorded at Muscle Shoals Sound were Bob Dylan, Dire Straits, Duane Allman, Wilson Pickett, Bob Seger, Paul Simon, the Staple Singers, Rod Stewart, Lynyrd Skynyrd, and Cher. Jimmy Johnson said, "We'd get a new artist every Monday morning. We were doing fifty albums a year."

From 1969 to 1971, a talented guitarist named Eddie Hinton joined the session musicians at the Jackson Highway studio. He was known for his distinctive leads by the likes of Aretha Franklin, Johnnie Taylor, the Staple Singers, Elvis Presley, and Wilson Pickett. But Hinton was far more than a guitar player. He was a masterful songwriter who penned songs for Percy Sledge, Dusty Springfield, Bobby Womack, and Chrissie Hynde. He also possessed a soulful voice that one could mistake for Otis Redding were it not for Hinton's unique phrasing. Eddie was a talented arranger and producer as well.

Hinton often collaborated with songwriters, Donnie Fritts, Marlin Green, and Dan Penn.

Eddie Hinton was born on June 15, 1944, in Jacksonville, Florida.

Eddie's grandfather, Pryde Hinton, was a Church of Christ preacher who influenced Eddie's Delta blues style, and who would deliver religious-style oratory on Eddie's song, *Dear Y'all*.

Eddie attended the University of Alabama but dropped out to pursue his musical interests. After performing with a number of Tuscaloosa area bands in the 1960s, he met and collaborated with Duane and Gregg Allman.

The Allman Brothers tried to recruit him, but Eddie remained in Muscle Shoals where he continued to work as a session musician and songwriter.

Eddie's style was described as sparse, perfect, and unconventional. Other musicians admired his genius. One producer, Jim Dickinson, actually broke down in tears while watching Eddie play on *Freedom Train*.

Those who knew Eddie described him as an intense soul. Before shows, his vocal warm-ups often frightened those unaccustomed to him. Grunts, growls, and bluesy shouts could be heard echoing through studios and backstage areas.

It was widely believed that Eddie Hinton would be the "next big thing."

But in a time when Disco began to dominate the airwaves, Eddie's soulful Southern sound was almost criminally overlooked by the masses.

In *Remembering Eddie Hinton*, an article by Dick Cooper, Jim Dickinson is quoted as saying, "The business broke his heart. You can hear it if you listen to the records. But you can also hear the endurance…He just became like Van Gogh. There was this monumental genius. I never saw anyone take it further than Eddie."

Sadly, July 28, 1995, Eddie Hinton suffered a heart attack and passed away at the age of fifty-one. He was buried in Tuscaloosa.

But there are those who say his spirit still dwells within the walls of the recording studio at 3614 Jackson Highway.

The Muscle Shoals Sound Studio is now owned by the Muscle Shoals Music Foundation and is open for tours. Almost all visitors have felt the presence of something otherworldly in the building.

Many describe the sensation of chills sweeping over their body when they stand in the spot where the guitarists recorded.

Artists waiting to record claim to have glimpsed a man in a blue suit, standing in the building when no one else was supposed to be inside. Those who attended Eddie's funeral say he was buried in a blue suit.

Lights mysteriously dim in the bathroom where Eddie was fond of recording guitar parts.

One engineer claimed to have heard an entire band bring equipment into the building and then leave, but upon investigation, he saw no one and no gear.

Photographs have been known to fall off their display stands with no explanation.

In 2009, the Black Keys, hoping to recapture the studio's legendary sound, decided to record their album *Brothers* in the historic studio. *Brothers* would be the first album in thirty years to be recorded at Muscle Shoals Sound.

Since all the original equipment had been moved to the studio's expanded location in 1979, the Black Keys brought their own. On August 16, 2009, they arrived in Sheffield, hoping that "fingerprint sound" of Muscle Shoals would reveal itself.

However, more than the legendary sound materialized.

The band experienced burned out microphones. Lights in the building blinked on and off, and power surges fried some of their equipment. Producer and engineer, Mark Neill, blamed the technical difficulties on the ghosts he believes haunts the studio. "We went there for inspiration and, by God, we got it. In spades and ghosts."

The Black Keys' Dan Auerbach says *Brothers* is deeper all around than their previous albums, and attributes it to having recorded in the historic studio.

During a period of burnout, musician, Richard Young, of the Kentucky Headhunters, also encountered the spirit of Eddie Hinton. After a friend passed him a copy of Eddie's *Dear Y'all*, Young was inspired. "I don't know how I had missed out on it, but that album did more to fire me up to do whatever it was that I brought to that band on this album than anything! I would not have been able to do it without Eddie Hinton. It was like his ghost was present. It reinstated my faith that a white boy has got soul, too. It just tore me up. Now, I might not be able to sing with the heart he's got but I am sure gonna try. I guess his ghost actually snapped me out of it and put me back to square one where I want to be."

Bathroom where Eddie Hinton was fond of writing guitar parts and where Keith Richards wrote Wild Horses

Eddie Hinton was posthumously awarded a bronze star and recognized by the Alabama Music Hall of Fame in 2001. He continues to be known as one of the original pioneers of the Muscle Shoals music legacy.

Even today, tourists coming to the studio are often overcome with emotion upon entering the space where song after hit song was recorded. Many attest to feeling effervescent chills sweep over them as they peruse the space and the photographs of several of the artists who made the memorable music.

One Native American visitor claimed to sense an *energy* in the building that he refused to label as a ghostly haunting.

Whether or not Eddie Hinton's spirit resides in the celebrated studio, there's definitely *something* magical, an ethereal, musical footprint left behind by every soul who created, listened to, and appreciated the wonderful songs produced there.

THE CURSE OF THE RIVER SERPENT

Are there monsters in our midst?

Legends of enormous fish the size of Volkswagen Beetles have flourished in the cities and towns along the Tennessee River since the river was dammed by the Tennessee Valley Authority in the 1930s, and even before.

The 652 mile-long Tennessee River meanders through the Tennessee Valley, forming in Knoxville before emptying into the Ohio River at Paducah, Kentucky. Prior to pioneers settling the Tennessee Valley, the waterway was known as the Cherokee River because so many from that tribe had settled along its banks.

The word Tennessee, in fact, has its origins in the name of a Cherokee village: *Tanasi*. Since the first humans made their homes along its banks, the river has served as a major highway to transport goods and supplies between villages and towns.

As settlers moved into the area, hamlets sprang up along the river and its tributaries, and with those new communities, frightening tales of monstrous fish and slimy river serpents.

Bluffs and deep holes near river bends are perfect hiding places for blue catfish, flatheads, and channel cats. Some of the largest are believed to be in excess of twenty years old.

Mike Mitchell of Albertville, Alabama hooked a 102 pound blue cat, 54 inches long with a girth of 40 inches on Wheeler Lake. The largest on record weighed in at 111 pounds and was caught by Bill McKinley in 1996. Just to compare, these catzillas were more along the size of manatees than an average catfish.

Tales are often told about divers who refuse to go back in the water near Wilson Dam because of catfish so large they can swallow a man whole.

Fish tale? Or early photoshopping? You decide

TVA retiree, John P. Blackwell, was interviewed by Dennis Sherer in an article for the *Times Daily* on June 19, 2010. Though Blackwell says he never encountered such a fish, nor spoke to anyone who had, he told Sherer, "Even if there were giant catfish living around the dam, I doubt if anyone would ever actually see one. If you go down more than ten feet in the Tennessee River, it's pitch-black dark. You can't even see your hand in front of your face."

Catzilla caught in Tennessee River

Other divers he'd interviewed reported being bumped by large fish, but the black waters prevented them from seeing exactly what type creature they'd encountered.

And yet, myths of river monsters have circulated since the time when Cherokees inhabited the land.

Chief John Brown, an innkeeper and ferry operator at Moccasin Bend on the Tennessee River near Chattanooga, regaled his guests, mostly drovers moving herds of horses, mules, and cattle, with Cherokee legends of a witch who possessed a long, sharp finger she used to carve out children's livers, of underground panthers, and of a giant named Tsulkala. Often, Brown would invite his guests to walk the riverbank with him where he would tell them his favorite *Tanasi* story.

Brown recounted tales of water cannibals, haunted whirlpools, and of course, of a giant fish known as Dakwa.

Brown's Tavern near Chattanooga

"Dakwa has barbs at both sides of his mouth, like a catfish," Brown told his guests. "The barbs are scarlet. All man-killers have red at their mouths."

Brown would then point out a spot in the river and go on to tell the story of a Cherokee brave who was crossing there in his canoe when Dakwa rose up from the depths, hit the boat with such force that it sent the brave flying up into the air. When the warrior plummeted back down, Dakwa was there, mouth open wide enough to swallow the man whole.

The brave tried to slice his way out of Dakwa's belly with a mussel shell, but this irritated the fish who coughed the man up and spat him out on the bank. Dakwa, it is told, was so shamed at being defeated, he swam to the bottom of the river and mired himself in the mud—where he remains to this day.

Some fifty years after Brown's death on February 3, 1822, river dredging operations where his ferry had been, yielded a line of decomposing wagons that stretched from one side of the river to the other. Among the wagon parts lay human remains.

It is said that the site of Brown's ferry crossing can be seen from atop Lookout Mountain, and that sometimes a large creature is visible gliding through the water just beneath the otherwise placid surface.

Haunted John Brown's Tavern, near Chattanooga

John Brown's tavern is said to be haunted as well, perhaps by the many travelers who were said to have checked in, but never left.

Mysterious bloodstains still mar the upstairs floor and staircase. Those who lived in the valley below maintained that lights could be seen in the north end room, even when the house was supposed to be vacant. They claimed the sound of chains being dragged up and down the stairs could be heard, and inexplicable thuds thumped the floorboards as if a lifeless body had been let fall. Sleepers have been awakened by startling noises only to report seeing a glistening tomahawk floating in the darkness. For many years, locals hurried their teams when passing the house at night in their wagons.

Perhaps the ghosts there are those of murdered travelers—or possibly the wandering spirits of Dakwa's victims.

Early photo of gorge where river serpent was spotted

Dakwa isn't the only creature lurking in the murky depths of the Tennessee River.

Early in 1822, a farmer named Buck Sutton sat fishing on the banks of the Tennessee River in an area known as Van's Hole when he saw something strange moving through the water. Sutton shot to his feet to get a better view of what he described as a "monstrous fish" thrashing in the shallows less than three yards from the bank.

"It was the creature. I could see the thing, clear as day," he told his friends.

But this was no festive fish tale Sutton recounted. He'd heard stories about the cursed serpent of the Tennessee River, and how one look upon the ungodly beast portended the observer's assured doom.

True to the curse, Sutton died two days later.

In 1827, another man, Billy Burns, crossed the river very near where Sutton had encountered the creature. He claimed that some kind of "snake-like thing" rammed his canoe, nearly capsizing him.

Burns described the canoe-long serpent as being blue and yellow. The following summer, Burns, too, fell victim to the curse of the river serpent. *The Chattanooga Daily Commercial* reported that he'd "died in some strange manner."

In 1829, Jim Windom, another Chattanooga farmer, was fishing in Van's Hole when he witnessed a "monstrous head" rise out of the water. "It was less than ten feet away. It slowly passed me, then rolled over on its side."

Windom claimed the serpent circled his boat several times before he summoned the courage to paddle to shore. Windom described the creature as having a tall, black fin that protruded two feet above the water, and that its back measured a full two feet in width.

Horrified that he would fall victim to the curse, he began attending church, but that very autumn, he was stricken with a mysterious fever and died.

Native Americans have passed down stories of the creature, and how it attacked canoes and fishermen. All the tales bore similarities. The creature was described as having a huge, two foot wide, dog-like head, and a serpentine body at least twenty-five feet in length. Some claimed it possessed frothing lips and a black fin that rose from the center of its spiny back.

It was said the creature would disappear for months at a time, and it was believed that it traveled widely, visiting other parts of the Tennessee River—including the Shoals.

Curiously, a similar creature has been spotted in Lake Guntersville, and also in the Coosa River.

During the 1830s, there were several sightings of the serpent in the Tennessee River, though none seemed to end in premature death.

Sallie Wilson claimed to have seen the beast several times. Her husband professed to have encountered it on the south side of the river near Chickamauga Island. "It was in a playful mood," he recounted. "Its back fin was a foot and half out of the water and it left a frothy serpentine wake behind. When disturbed, it darted with incredible speed, and was no more than a minute in crossing the river."

Tales of the creature, and its supernatural powers, outlasted the sightings. The stories were whispered wherever fisherman and settlers gathered, around campfires, and along the swampy banks and in hidden sloughs.

The legend of the serpent reached as far as the *New York Times* in a March 13, 1888 story headlined: *The Sea Serpent in the Tennessee*. "A fishing party of four men report a novel and dangerous experience in the Tennessee River, a few miles below this place. (Knoxville) This afternoon, while crossing in a yawl, a serpent-like fish, fully ten feet in length, capsized the boat and threw all the men in the water. The boat was lashed to pieces and the men barely escaped with their lives."

Evidence does exist of an actual Alabama water serpent. It was called zeuglodon, and was a prehistoric whale that grew to about seventy feet in length. Real fossilized remains were found about the same time stories of the Tennessee River serpent surfaced.

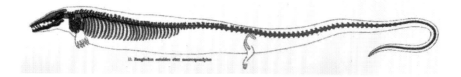

Zeugloden

A full skeleton of a zeuglodon resides in the Alabama Museum of Natural History in Tuscaloosa, Alabama. In 1984, the state Legislature passed an act naming the remains the state fossil.

Fossilized specimens of zeuglodons are still found today and are protected by law.

But could zeuglodon, like the alligator, have adapted and survived the eons to terrorize the waters in the Tennessee Valley?

As deep and dark as the Tennessee River lakes have become, we may never know what prehistoric creatures might still lurk in the underwater caves and muddy depths in which we fish, boat—and swim.

THE GHOST OF HIGHWAY 5

The small town of Lynn, Alabama in Winston County, boasts a population of around 600. The town was incorporated in 1952, and is supported by several small businesses and a mobile home manufacturing company.

Lynn's history stretches back to antebellum Alabama, when a post office was established in nearby Larissa on May 6, 1857.

The first postmaster was Andrew Jackson Ingle, who would later become a founding father of Double Springs. After the Civil War, the post office was relocated to Lynn and reopened August 1, 1888.

Before the town was dubbed Lynn, it was known as Black Swamp, a name used in the 1900 census.

In 1889, John White Lynn donated land for railroad right-of-way, along with property for a depot, and thus Black Swamp became Lynn.

Lynn's crime rate is far below the national average. Therefore, it's difficult to imagine the sleepy Southern town is home to a restless spirit.

Lynn is bisected by a narrow, two-lane road known as Highway 5.

Legend states that a woman, attending a race at the Winston County Drag Strip, got into a fight with her husband and decided to walk home.

Darkness blanketed the lonely highway, a foggy mist further hampering visibility.

And when an eighteen-wheeler coal truck barreled by, the driver inadvertently struck and killed the woman.

Ever since that fateful night, truckers along Highway 5, have had encounters with the terrifying apparition of a woman bent on revenge.

A trucker named Eddie maintains that in 1994, while driving down Highway 5, the ghostly woman banged on his truck door, demanding to know if he was responsible for her murder.

One driver, named Michael, said his encounter with the ghost of Highway 5 made a believer out of him.

Another, named Derrick, claims to have seen the phantom woman standing on the side of the road near the old drag strip entrance.

A different trucker had a far more horrifying experience.

Late one night, while driving Highway 5, his headlights shone on a figure standing in the middle of the road. He braked his truck and managed to stop before hitting the woman.

For several tense seconds she stood in the glare of his headlights, staring at him, and then all of a sudden, the woman appeared in front of his gear shift, peering hard to see if he was the driver responsible for ending her life.

The driver went out of his way to avoid Highway 5 at night after that.

RESTLESS SPIRITS IN THE MCREYNOLDS HOUSE

At the time of the Civil War, Tuscumbia, Alabama became a strategic military target. Situated on the railroad, in close proximity to Corinth, Mississippi, and Pittsburgh Landing (Shiloh), Tuscumbia was one of Alabama's most prosperous cities.

After the Battle of Shiloh, Tuscumbia was occupied by Union officer, John Basil Turchin (1822-1901). Turchin was infamous for the "Sack of Athens," Alabama on May 2, 1862, shortly after his occupation of Tuscumbia.

Turchin would later face disciplinary action for plundering houses, destroying personal property, burning buildings, and tearing down fences. However, Turchin's connections garnered him a promotion to Brigadier General, and his harsh treatment of Southern civilians was lauded by US Secretary of War, Edwin Stanton.

Turchin's approach would later be emulated by General William Tecumseh Sherman during his notorious "March to the Sea."

Turchin, however, wasn't the most destructive officer to invade the Tennessee Valley. Federal commander of the 10th Missouri Cavalry, Colonel Florence Cornyn, and his outfit known as the "Destroying Angels," left the area devastated.

John Basil Turchin

On April 28, 1863, Cornyn burned LaGrange College, then extoled as the West Point of the South, and the first institution of higher learning in the state. He went on to fire granaries, mills, barns, and even as many as a hundred homes.

After Cornyn's ruthless raid, Lieutenant William D. Bowen, his second in command, pressed charges against Cornyn. During the court-martial proceedings held in Corinth, Mississippi on August 10, 1863, Bowen approached Cornyn. The confrontation was most likely due to the fact that authorities tried to cover up Cornyn's use of excessive force against civilians.

The two engaged in a verbal altercation which quickly accelerated into a fistfight. Bowen knocked Cornyn to the floor, drew his pistol and fired five shots into his former commanding officer, killing him.

Lieutenant Bowen was first acquitted of Cornyn's murder, though the verdict was overturned and Bowen was dismissed from duty and spent nine months in prison.

Among the homes destroyed in the 1863 raid, was the McReynolds Home about five miles east of Tuscumbia.

Robert S. McReynolds and his wife, Mary Hogan McReynolds,

relocated their young family to one of the slave cabins on their plantation. But even there, and after the war's end, they would not be safe from the marauding Federal Army.

10th Missouri Cavalry Colonel Florence M. Cornyn

Mary McReynolds recorded an account of the Union Army's return to her doorstep on their way from Corinth, Mississippi, where Confederate General Joe Johnston had surrendered, to Decatur, Alabama. "The railroad having been destroyed, their route brought them to my home. Early on the morning of the Fourth of July, 1865, I became the mother of an infant, and before the babe was three hours old, the Yankee soldiers began pouring into the room I occupied, a very small slave cabin, our dwelling, barn, corncrib, etc., all having been burned in 1863 by the same Yankees. From 9 a.m. to 8 p.m. they were unwelcome guests. My husband tried all his persuasive powers to keep them from coming into my room, telling them I was sick, weak, and nervous. Their reply was always the same thing. 'Can't help it.' 'We want to see the damn little Rebel!'"

LaGrange College

The McReynolds family apparently recovered throughout the tough Reconstruction Era years. In 1880, they built a two-story frame Queen Anne house with a hipped roof, projecting gables, and welcoming front porch decorated with Victorian style brackets and spindle work, at 509 Main Street, in Tuscumbia, Alabama.

Robert McReynolds died only ten years after relocating to Main Street, on February 23, 1890.

Mary McReynolds passed away at the age of 90, on May 13, 1926. They are buried in Oakwood Cemetery in Tuscumbia.

At the time of Mary McReynolds' death, at least one of their adult children was living in the 509 Main Street house. In 1920, a man, interestingly named William Bowen, rented part of the house as a boarder or for use as an office space. His profession is listed as bookkeeper, and it is not known whether he bore any relation to the Lieutenant William Bowen who assassinated Florence Cornyn.

Lieutenant William D. Bowen

In the 1960s, the stately Victorian McReynolds House became home to the WVNA radio station. Though WVNA ceased broadcasting in 2014, the other satellite stations, including Rock 105.5, continue to air. The cluster of stations now belongs to Urban Radio.

But since the house was converted for use as the radio station, employees there have reported several eerie encounters with a ghostly presence.

DJs working the overnight shift alone often hear footsteps on the stairs, and the sound of chairs being dragged across the second floor.

One former Marine called then program director, David Havens, around three in the morning, to tell him that something was going on upstairs, that he could hear someone walking the floors. The ex-Marine checked, but found no one there. When he returned downstairs, the noises started again. He quit three days later.

David believed him, because he, too, had experienced the haunting. On several occasions, he'd heard the unexplained footsteps, and had witnessed the business phone indicator lighting up to let someone know the line was in use. But whenever he picked up the phone, knowing no one else was in the building, all he got was a dial tone.

McReynolds House, 509 N. Main Street, Tuscumbia

A particular bathroom door would often creak open of its own accord, making an unnerving noise in the otherwise quiet house.

Another employee, Jennifer George, who worked mostly

weekends at the station, covered one overnight shift before refusing those hours again. With good reason.

When she stepped out of the FM control room, that fateful night, she saw the faded apparition of a man, clad in a blue shirt, walking across the hall, toward the exit that led to the old well house.

All during the night, footsteps came from the second story, chairs shifted across the floorboards, doors opened and closed, and like David, she witnessed the phones lighting up as if someone were trying to make a call.

When Jennifer related her story to some of the other employees, they admitted that they'd had similar experiences in the house. Some had even seen the spirit of the blue-shirt clad man.

The activity wasn't limited to the overnight hours.

When the house was otherwise quiet, and Jennifer was the only employee present, she often heard the sounds of a presence milling about upstairs.

Many assumed the ghost or ghosts haunting the McReynolds House originated from the Yellow Fever epidemic of 1878.

Though many lives were claimed throughout the nineteenth century by the dread disease, 1878 was by far the worst for Tuscumbians.

The 1878 outbreak was responsible for 20,000 deaths throughout the Mississippi River Valley, and reached Tuscumbia by way of refugees from Memphis who arrived in North Alabama, carrying the disease.

About 100 Shoals area inhabitants fell victim to the epidemic, thirty-one of those in Tuscumbia. One in three diagnosed with the disease died from it.

A few isolated cases were reported in 1879, and again in 1888, though no more epidemics occurred.

A historic marker stands near the house at 509 N. Main Street, that bears the names of the victims.

Since the McReynolds House wasn't built until two years after the epidemic, it is unlikely the house served as a Yellow Fever hospital, as was widely believed, though most certainly the neighboring houses could have been used to house the sick.

Another legend that circulated about the McReynolds House maintains that a little girl was killed catching a school bus in front of the building. Some amateur ghost hunters believe they confirmed this story in 1998, but no hard evidence has been produced.

Those who continue to work in the building may never know the identity of the soul responsible for the unsettling noises that occur both day and night in the station, but they know one thing for sure.

The historic Victorian house, on the beautiful, tree-lined, Southern street, is definitely haunted.

A GHOSTLY VISITOR TO THE ROUNDHOUSE

Tuscumbia is one of the oldest towns in Alabama. Even today, descendants of the first settlers dwell in the many historic houses, shaded by ancient oaks.

Some of the first pioneers to the area were French traders who established a trading post at the mouth of the Occocoposo, or Cold Water Creek, in the 1780s.

The creek, which runs through the town, is the outlet for a massive spring that originates near the center of Tuscumbia and flows toward the Tennessee River, two miles to the north.

In 1787, Colonel James Robertson organized an expedition to the area. He attacked and defeated the Native American settlement and its French allies, and claimed the trading post.

By 1802, a treaty had been signed with the Chickasaws to cut a wagon road, some twenty miles southwest of Tuscumbia, that stretched from Natchez, Mississippi to Nashville, Tennessee. This wagon road would later be called the Natchez Trace.

As more and more white settlers migrated to the area, additional treaties were signed by General Andrew Jackson and Colonel Benjamin Hawkins to secure the lands. By 1816, the Native

Americans had granted all the territory from the mouth of the Coosa River to Cotton Gin Port, Mississippi, encompassing present-day Tuscumbia.

In October 1819, a bill was passed to name the settlement Big Spring. The following year, the name was changed to that of a renowned Chickasaw chief—Tuscumbia.

When Congress passed the Indian Removal Act in 1830, around one-hundred thousand Native Americans were forced to leave their homes on a brutal trek to Oklahoma that spanned twenty years. Their journey would become known as the Trail of Tears.

The first railroad west of the Alleghany Mountains was the one from Tuscumbia to the Tennessee River. Completed in 1832, it was roughly two miles in length. In 1834, it merged with the Tuscumbia & Decatur Railroad, and was used mainly to transport cotton to steamers bound for New Orleans, Ohio, and St. Louis.

By 1857, the Memphis & Charleston Railroad connected with the Tuscumbia & Decatur Road, making it the first in the United States to link the Atlantic Ocean with the Mississippi River.

Being the only east-west railroad, the line became of strategic importance during the Civil War.

During the nineteenth century, trains ran from 1857 through 1894, until the line was absorbed by Southern Railway.

Before the Tennessee Valley Authority dammed the Tennessee River, rail transport was the only means of getting goods past the treacherous shoals.

During its railroad heyday, Tuscumbia boasted three depots. Trains running down Railroad Street (present-day 5th St.), would stop at hotels and businesses along Commercial Row, delivering goods and passengers.

The last depot was constructed in 1888, by the Memphis & Charleston Railroad. Adjacent was a repair shop known as the roundhouse, where trains, which at that time had no reverse gear, could be turned around on a turntable that was operated by a single employee.

While browsing nineteenth century copies of a Tuscumbia

newspaper, area native and historian, John McWilliams, came across an intriguing advertisement placed by the Memphis & Charleston Railroad.

According to McWilliams' research, late one night, as a train rumbled into town from Memphis, it struck a man who was either sleeping, or had been murdered and placed, on the tracks near the Spring Creek bridge.

Spring Creek Bridge

The man was so mangled no one was able to identify him. Since it could not be determined whether he'd been murdered prior to being hit by the train, the case was closed, and the man was buried in a graved marked *Unknown*.

Shortly thereafter, several Tuscumbians witnessed a ghostly man making his way up the tracks from Spring Creek toward the rail yard. The spirit entered the roundhouse, begging for help from employees who were busy readying an engine for a run.

When the battered-looking apparition suddenly vanished, the men raced out of the roundhouse. The engine began to roll, nearly killing an employee who was cleaning the ash pan.

The ghostly visits began to occur on a regular basis, terrifying the men in the shop. In response, the Memphis & Charleston Railroad placed an advertisement in several newspapers requesting the help of an exorcist.

The ads stopped, but apparently, the haunting still continues.

In 2010, video evidence yielded a shadowy figure opening a door in the depot that, it is said, can never be locked. The specter walked through the door, and into the room.

The 1888 depot is now fully restored and houses the Tuscumbia Railway Museum. A replica roundhouse was constructed in 2013. The museum at 205 West Fifth Street, in Tuscumbia is open for tours, and the depot is a stop on Tuscumbia's History and Haunts Trolley Tour.

If you happen to tour the museum, look closely. The ghost of the mangled victim might just make an appearance.

The New Roundhouse Event Center at the historic Tuscumbia Depot

Historic Tuscumbia Depot

I WILL RETURN SOON

The most famous ghost of Athens State University is that of the haunting beauty, Abigail Lylia Burns. Students, staff, and faculty alike have observed a shadowy figure holding a bouquet of roses and peering from a third floor window of McCandless Hall.

Her story is one of unrequited love – and tragedy.

Legend holds that Abigail Burns was an up-and-coming opera singer from Philadelphia, who had befriended the Institution's president in the early 1900s. While visiting the campus, the striking and talented singer met one of Athens' handsome young attorneys. For the pair, it was love at first sight.

Every day, the two would secretly meet in the art studio on the third floor of McCandless Hall, the elegant Greek Revival building with its auditorium where she would later perform her final recital.

On November 12, the last night of Abigail's visit to Athens, she sang selections from Verdi's opera *La Traviata* to the enthralled students and guests in McCandless' auditorium. The crowd adored her and, at the end of her performance, graced her with a bouquet of red roses. Abigail made a vow. "I will return soon."

McCandless Hall, early 1900s

As soon as she left the stage, she rendezvoused with her newfound love for one final time in the art studio, and there after pledging her undying love to him, she reiterated her promise to him. "I will return soon."

But that night, her horse drawn carriage was caught in a terrible storm. Frightened, the driver decided to stop and wait out the deluge of rain. He searched frantically for a safe place to park the carriage, however, none could be found. Instead, the driver came upon a bridge.

Lightning flashed. Thunder boomed. The horses reared and bolted, disengaging the carriage. In haste, the driver abandoned the rig, but too terrified to get out, Abigail remained inside as it careened over the rail and crashed onto the rocks below.

The driver scurried to where Abigail lay, mortally wounded, still clutching her bouquet of red roses. There, Abigail gasped her last words. "I've a promise to keep. I must return."

Not long after her death, Abigail fulfilled her promise.

Witnesses began seeing the apparition of a beautiful woman,

clutching a bouquet of roses, in the window of the art studio and also on the stage where she last performed in McCandless Hall.

The scent of roses is detected even when no flowers are present. Some students have seen the ghost of a woman in the dressing room, preparing for a performance. Often, the footsteps of slippered feet can be heard traversing the floors of the stately building.

In memory of her, a hackberry tree was planted just to the side of McCandless Hall where it still stands sentinel today.

Those who pass by on the anniversary of Abigail's death, will most assuredly see the apparition of a beautiful woman, clutching a bouquet of red roses, as she peers out the window in search of her long lost love.

McCandless Hall, early 1900s

A HAUNTING ON HAWTHORNE STREET

Beneath the shade of ancient oak trees, a historic marker stands at the intersection of North Wood Avenue and West Hawthorne Street observing the stately Queen Anne and Georgian Revival homes and some of their locally famous inhabitants.

Pulitzer Prize winning author, Tom Stribling, Chief Engineer of the Panama Canal, George Goethals, and Helen Keller, were among those who resided in the Wood Avenue historic district.

Walking through the neighborhood is like taking a voyage back in time. Very little has changed in the area since the early 1900s. Gazing up at the labyrinth of tree limbs overhead, and traversing the sidewalks amidst the elaborate Victorian houses with their shingled siding, turned and carved ornamentation, and turrets, it is easy to imagine what it would have been like when horses and buggies jostled along the streets.

Though most of the homes date from after the Reconstruction Era, at least five stood during the antebellum period.

When University of North Alabama student, Brooke Sizemore, moved into her apartment at 226 East Hawthorne Street, in downtown Florence, Alabama, she thought she was embarking on an exciting, educational journey.

She didn't expect to encounter the preternatural presence of the historic home's former occupant.

Mitchell Malone House, circa 1915

In the 2010s, she moved into apartment 1 with her friend, Alex. They were thrilled to find affordable housing, just steps from campus. But almost from the very first day, strange things began to happen.

Nearly every night, Brooke was awakened as her bedroom doorknob turned, followed by the unmistakable groaning of the old hinges as the door slowly swung open.

On more than one occasion, she and Alex both found a kitchen chair turned upside down when no one had been in the room. Sometimes they actually witnessed the chair toppling over without being touched—by human hands, that is.

Out of the corner of her eye, Brooke often saw a shadowy figure moving through the hall.

Cold drafts circulated through the apartment, even in the dead of summer.

And Brooke, who'd experienced visits in prophetic dreams from a grandmother who'd passed away several years before her birth, sensed the spirit in the Hawthorne Street house was attempting to communicate with her.

She felt the ghost was that of a benevolent doctor, and that she reminded him of his wife.

But as the ghost's attempts to get her attention increased in strength and intensity, Brooke responded to a request for people with paranormal ability from MTV's *True Life*, a series which follows three young adults in their everyday lives, to document the problems and goals they face.

MTV agreed to film Brooke as a part of the series, in an episode called *True Life: I Have Paranormal Ability*.

The producer introduced Brooke to Deborah Collard, a psychic based in South Alabama, who confirmed Brooke's intuition that the spirit was that of a doctor who'd served patients in the house.

They believed the spirit had somehow become trapped between worlds and needed their assistance to move on.

The MTV producer also connected Brooke with local historians who did some research on the 226 East Hawthorne Street house.

During the 1860s, the area of town north of the University of North Alabama campus was mostly wooded. In this rural area was, among others, the 1830s Mitchell / Redd house at 747 North Wood Avenue, the 1859 Ashcraft House at 803 Meridian Street, and the Reverend Mitchell Malone house at 226 East Hawthorne Street.

Evidence suggests that Mitchell Malone, Sr. built or bought the house on Hawthorne Street when he moved to Florence from Tuscumbia. Some believe the original structure could date back to the 1830s.

The senior Malone's son, Reverend Mitchell Malone, was born near Dixon in Colbert County, Alabama, August 13, 1842. The fifth of twelve children, he was educated at Montaclaux Academy in Lauderdale County, and at Wesleyan University from 1858 to 1861, when at the first call for volunteers, he enlisted in the Florence Guards, the first company to leave the county for war. For one year, he served in Company K of the Seventh Alabama Infantry, and for the remainder of the war, in Company F, Fourth Alabama Cavalry, where he attained the rank of sergeant-major.

While Mitchell Malone saw action, the Civil War reached Alabama in the early months of 1862, when Grant captured Forts Henry and Donelson on the Tennessee River. February saw the arrival of Federal gunboats in Florence.

Reverend Mitchell Malone, Jr.

By March, Grant had his gunboats positioned at Pittsburgh Landing near Savannah, Tennessee, where he planned to attack Confederate General Albert Sidney Johnston's Army of Tennessee that was encamped at Corinth, Mississippi.

When the two armies clashed at Shiloh Church, April 6th and 7th, 1862, each side took approximately ten thousand casualties.

Many of those wounded during the early months of 1862, were brought to Florence to convalesce, and it is believed the Malone house served as one of the first Civil War hospitals. Other field hospitals were located at the Elliott Hotel on South Court Street, the old Webb/Fant factory building on the corner of Court and Alabama Streets, some warehouses at the wharf, and Pope's Tavern.

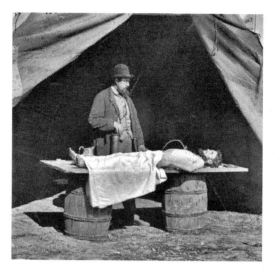

A deceased Civil War soldier being embalmed

After the war, Mitchell Malone returned to the area, and on March 24, 1868, he married Eliza J. Walston. On October 28, 1880, he was licensed to preach in the Methodist Episcopal Church South.

In 1896, he was elected assessor of Lauderdale County and served a second term in 1900.

The 1910 and 1920 censuses show the family residing on Hawthorne Street. Mitchell Malone died, at the age of eighty-four on February 3, 1927, in Florence. He is buried in the Florence Cemetery.

In 1930, Malone's widow, Eliza, still lived at the address. She passed away February 5, 1931, at the age of eighty.

According to late Florence Historian, William L. McDonald, in his book *A Walk Through the Past: People and Places of Florence and Lauderdale County*, the Malone house would again serve Florence as a public hospital following the war years. But new research has indicated that in May of 1900, the Florence Public Hospital was established near Saint Joseph Catholic Church in an area then known as Lawton

Heights, in a house once owned by Dr. James Boardman Hawthorne, Baptist minister and president of the Baptist University that opened on Seymour Street near the old stone water tower.

It is believed the Malone house served as a hotel sometime in the twentieth century.

Mitchell Malone

Eliza Walston Malone

In the early 80s, the structure was converted for use as apartments, mainly catering to University of North Alabama students. Many students housed in the Hawthorne Street apartments have reported inexplicable and eerie occurrences.

And if the house was used as a Civil War field hospital, there are likely more spirits who wander through the rooms and halls of the apartments on Hawthorne Street.

GHOST OF THE GOLDEN HORSE

The Natchez Trace stretches approximately 440 miles from Natchez, Mississippi to Nashville, Tennessee. Forged nearly ten thousand years ago by Native Americans, the Trace was later traveled by early explorers, traders, and settlers in the late 18th and early 19th centuries.

Today, the Natchez Trace Parkway closely follows the original path, and visitors can enjoy a scenic drive, as well as hiking, biking, horseback riding, and even camping.

The first documented explorer on the trail was a Frenchman who, in 1742, with Native American guides, wrote of the "miserable conditions."

Eager to connect the Mississippi frontier to the more settled areas of the country, Thomas Jefferson authorized a postal road to be constructed between Daniel Boone's Wilderness Road, near Nashville, and the Mississippi River. After signing peace treaties with the Chickasaw and Choctaw tribes, development began for the "Columbian Highway."

By 1809, the trail was fully accessible by wagon.

But early transit along the Trace was fraught with danger from the elements and by those who intended to waylay and rob unsuspecting travelers.

Several inns, then known as *stands*, sprang up along the route.

One of those stands was operated by the second son of Scottish settler, James Logan Colbert, and his Chickasaw wife, Minta Hoye. His name was George "Tootemastubbe" Colbert.

George Colbert

George Colbert was born in present-day Alabama, and conflicting evidence indicates the year of his birth was 1764. He was believed to have serve the colonials during the American Revolution under Arthur St. Clair and Anthony Wayne.

Colbert married three times. Before 1797, he married Salechie, the daughter of Chief Doublehead. She died February 1, 1846. He took Sister Doublehead as a wife prior to 1807. She died in 1813 at Colbert Ferry, Alabama, and was buried in Colbert County. He married his third wife, Tuskeahooto, in 1834.

During his tenure in North Alabama, Colbert amassed several acres of fertile farmland, and he owned more than 150 slaves.

As more settlers poured into North Alabama, George Colbert established a ferry in the vicinity of Cherokee, Alabama, which he operated from 1800 to 1820. Those traveling the Trace could also enjoy a warm meal or the lodgings at Colbert's Stand.

Home of George Colbert

One guest wrote of eating a venison supper and then retiring to an outbuilding dubbed Wilderness Haven, which he shared with "not less than fifty Indians, many of them drunk."

A traveling preacher described George Colbert as "shrewd, talented, and wicked."

Where the Trace crossed the Tennessee River, the current was so strong, travelers referred to it as the most dangerous obstacle between Natchez and Nashville. Colbert charged his customers 50 cents per person to cross, $1.00 if they were on a horse, and 50 cents for every riderless horse. Though the travelers felt the fees were outrageous, they had little other choice than to pay or risk death trying to swim across the swift waters.

When Andrew Jackson and his army of Tennesseans arrived at Colbert's Ferry in 1815, as they returned from the War of 1812, George Colbert infamously charged them $75,000 to cross.

Jackson became so enraged, he drew his sword and whacked a chunk out of one of Colbert's porch posts.

The two men, however unlikely, became tenuous allies. During the Creek Wars, George Colbert assembled 350 Chickasaw warriors to fight alongside Andrew Jackson against the Red Sticks.

A typical frontier day ferry

But Jackson, it seems, wasn't the only disgruntled customer Colbert encountered.

One man arrived at the ferry on horseback, his saddlebags bulging with gold, and Colbert, who most likely noticed the full-to-bursting load, quoted him an exorbitant price to cross.

The two argued, but George, knowing the man had no choice but to pay, refused to come down on his price.

The man decided he would swim his horse across instead, and rider and beast plunged into the swift water. The already-weary horse struggled to swim against the mighty current, but it proved too much and the animal started to drown.

Legend maintains that Colbert poled his ferry out to help, telling the man to hand up the saddlebags. Suspecting he was about to be cheated by the shrewd Chickasaw, the man refused and he and the horse sank beneath the surface.

Though the corpses of the rider and horse were found downriver, the saddlebags were never recovered.

Since that time, travelers in the area have sighted the golden skeleton of a horse's head emerging from the water before disappearing back into the depths.

There are those who believe the ghost of the horse is still fighting the strong current, while others maintain the beast is guarding the gold for his master.

In the 1830s, George Colbert and his family were moved to Oklahoma under the Indian Removal Act. He took his 150 slaves with him, and established a farm near Fort Towson. He died there on

November 7, 1839.

Incidentally, in 1971, two men found a gold ingot, the size of a brick in the area where Colbert's ferry operated. And years earlier, a farmer working a field in the vicinity, discovered a gold bar.

Could this be evidence of the gold the ghost horse seeks to protect?

Today, a visitors' center, a picnic area, and riverside hiking trails commemorate the spot where Colbert operated his ferry and inn.

If you happen to visit, perhaps you will see the ghost of the golden horse, rising up from the deep, dark waters of the Tennessee River.

George Colbert's Home

PLACES OF INTEREST

Florence / Lauderdale Tourism
200 Jim Spain Drive
Florence, Alabama 35630
(256) 740-4141

Muscle Shoals Sound Studio
3614 N Jackson Hwy
Sheffield, Alabama
(256) 394-3562
Studio Tours: Mon — Thurs 10 – 2 pm, Fri—Sat 10 – 4

Bankhead National Forest
Double Springs, Alabama 35553
(205) 489-5111

Colbert Ferry / Natchez Trace Parkway
Milepost 327.3
www.natcheztracetravel.com

Historic Tuscumbia Railway Depot
204 W. 5th St
Tuscumbia, AL 35674
(256) 389-1357
Tues—Fri 9 am – 4 pm, Sat, 10 am – 3 pm

HAUNTED HISTORY OF THE SHOALS GHOST WALK TOUR

A spine chilling night awaits you in the company of a masterful storyteller who will entertain you with tales steeped in legend, folklore, and truth.

As twilight creeps over the homes and hidden courtyards of historic downtown Florence, prepare yourself to witness the mysterious and inexplicable.

Each year, during the week of Halloween, Debra conducts the Haunted History of the Shoals Ghost Walk Tour.

Souls depart at 7:30 pm, from Wilson Park in Historic Downtown Florence.

Tours last 90 minutes and cover approximately 1 mile.

Reservations are not required.

Visit www.FlorenceGhostWalk for more information, or to contact Debra.

Other Northwest Alabama Haunted Attractions:

Arx Mortis Haunted House
4051 Hwy. 72
Killen, AL 35645

WHERE DEBRA'S OTHER BOOKS CAN BE FOUND

Florence / Lauderdale Tourism
200 Jim Spain Drive
Florence, Alabama 35630
(256) 740-4141

Cold Water Bookstore
101 W. Sixth St
Tuscumbia, Alabama
(256) 381-2525

Ye Ole General Store
219 N Seminary St
Florence, Alabama 35630
(256) 764-0601

Lawrence County Archives
2588 Hwy 43 S
Leoma, TN 38468
(931) 852-4091

www.Amazon.com

ABOUT THE AUTHOR

DEBRA GLASS is the author of more than thirty five books. Since childhood she has been fascinated by things that go bump in the night. While writing True Shoals Ghost Stories Vol. 1, she realized many of the hauntings occurred in her hometown of Florence, Alabama, and decided to start a ghost walk tour. Since its beginnings in 2002, the Haunted History of the Shoals Ghost Walk Tour has become a perennial favorite during the Halloween season.

Debra lives in Alabama with her family, two smart-alec ghosts, and a glaring of diabolical black cats.

Other folklore collections by Debra Glass include:

True Shoals Ghost Stories Vol. 1

True Shoals Ghost Stories Vol. 2

Skeletons on Campus – True Ghost Stories of Alabama Colleges and Universities

Skeletons of the Civil War – True Ghost Stories of the Army of Tennessee

Haunted Mansions in the Heart of Dixie

Young Adult Paranormal Romance

Eternal

Debra conducts the Haunted History of the Shoals Ghost Walk Tour annually during the week of Halloween. For more information about Debra, her books, and her tour, check out her website: www.FlorenceGhostWalk.com

Made in the USA
Lexington, KY
11 September 2017